Text copyright © 1998 by William Kaplan
Original illustrations copyright © 1998 by Stephen Taylor

We acknowledge the financial assistance of the Canada Council
for the Arts, the Ontario Arts Council and the Government of
Canada through the Book Publishing Industry Development
Program for our publishing activities.

Groundwood Books / Douglas & McIntyre
585 Bloor Street West,
Toronto, Ontario M6G 1K5

Distributed in the U.S.A. by
Publishers Group West
1700 Fourth Street, Berkeley, CA 94710

Library of Congress data is available

Canadian Cataloguing in Publication Data

Kaplan, William, 1957-
One more border : the true story of one family's escape from
war-torn Europe

"A Groundwood book".
ISBN 0-88899-332-3

1. Kaplan family - Juvenile literature. 2. Kaplan, Igor - Juvenile
literature. 3. Refugees, Jewish - Lithuania - Biography - Juvenile
literature. 4. Jews - Lithuania - Biography - Juvenile literature. 5.
World War, 1939-1945 - personal narratives, Jewish - Juvenile
literature. I. Tanaka, Shelley. II. Taylor, Stephen, 1964- .
III. Title.

D804.196.K36 1998   j940.53'08691   C98-930853-7

Printed and bound in China by Everbest Printing Co. Ltd.

ONE MORE BORDER

A GROUNDWOOD BOOK

DOUGLAS & McINTYRE

VANCOUVER TORONTO BUFFALO

ONE MOR

THE TRUE STORY
OF ONE FAMILY'S ESCAPE
FROM WAR-TORN EUROPE

BORDER

WILLIAM KAPLAN

WITH SHELLEY TANAKA

ILLUSTRATED BY STEPHEN TAYLOR

"Nomi," Igor whispered, shaking his sister awake. "Get up!"

Nomi rolled over and rubbed her eyes. Her brother was dressed in his good trousers and jacket, the ones he wore to synagogue. Behind him, Mother and Father hurried past the door carrying clothes and large suitcases.

"I don't want to get up," Nomi said. "It's too early."

"But we have to leave Memel," Igor insisted, pulling at the blankets.
"The Nazis are coming to the city and they hate Jews."

"Why?" Nomi looked up at her older brother. Igor was tall and thin
and very smart. He knew everything.

But this time he just shook his head. "I don't know. But we have to go."

It was spring, 1939. Igor and Nomi had to leave almost everything behind, even their nanny, Gretchen. Igor closed his bedroom door on his books, his recorder, his football and his train set. He saw his mother take a last look at her paintings and piano. She'd already closed up her photography studio in town, leaving all her valuable equipment.

As the car pulled away, Igor gazed back at the house he had lived in all his life. It had a round turret, just like a castle. He saw the sea spray against the rocks and wondered if he would ever see his home again.

They drove farther and farther away from the sea until they reached Kaunas, the capital of Lithuania. Igor had never seen such a beautiful city. It had big buildings and wide, tree-lined streets.

They moved into a hotel in the center of town. Maids brought fresh towels each morning. Igor and Nomi had dessert at every meal in the hotel restaurant. They went to the local school. Best of all, Mother looked after them instead of Gretchen.

Bottom left:
Memel, 1938.

Bottom right:
Family fleeing Memel under the gaze of Nazi troops, 1939.

In the spring of 1939, Europe was on the brink of war. World War II would kill more people and cause more damage than any other war in history. More than fifty countries would take part, and its effects would be felt all over the world.

World War II was a complicated war with many causes, but one of them was Germany's desire to gain more territory. Its leader, Adolf Hitler, wanted to create one huge superpower ruled by German people. It would be a nation without Jews.

As Hitler's control spread over Europe, Jews were forced to leave their homes. Two days after Igor Kaplan and his family fled from their house by the sea, German troops seized Memel from Lithuania. Soldiers broke the windows of Nadja Kaplan's photography studio and took all of the family's possessions.

Top: German soldiers parade before Adolf Hitler.

Bottom: The invading German army marches through a burning town in Poland.

Left: The broken shop window of a Jewish-owned business.

Center: German soldiers watch as a synagogue burns.

Right: Jews are rounded up in Lithuania.

Nomi thought it was almost like being on holiday. But Igor heard his parents whispering late at night. He saw how his mother picked at her food, how Father stopped giving them money for candies in the hotel shop.

Then, in the fall, Germany invaded Poland, Lithuania's neighbor to the south. By the following summer, Russian troops had moved into Lithuania from the east, to protect their own frontier, they said.

Igor and Nomi stopped going to school. Igor saw letters arriving from Canada, where his grandparents had moved a few years before.

"Are we going to live in the hotel forever?" he asked his father. "Why aren't we going to school?"

"Russia controls Lithuania now," Father said. "They don't like the Jews any more than the Nazis do. They've closed our schools and synagogues and made it difficult for Jews to be Jews."

"Where can we go and still be Jews?"

His father put a hand on his shoulder. "We are going to try to go to Canada, where Oma and Opa live."

"Is Canada far?" Nomi asked.

"Yes," Father sighed. "Very, very far."

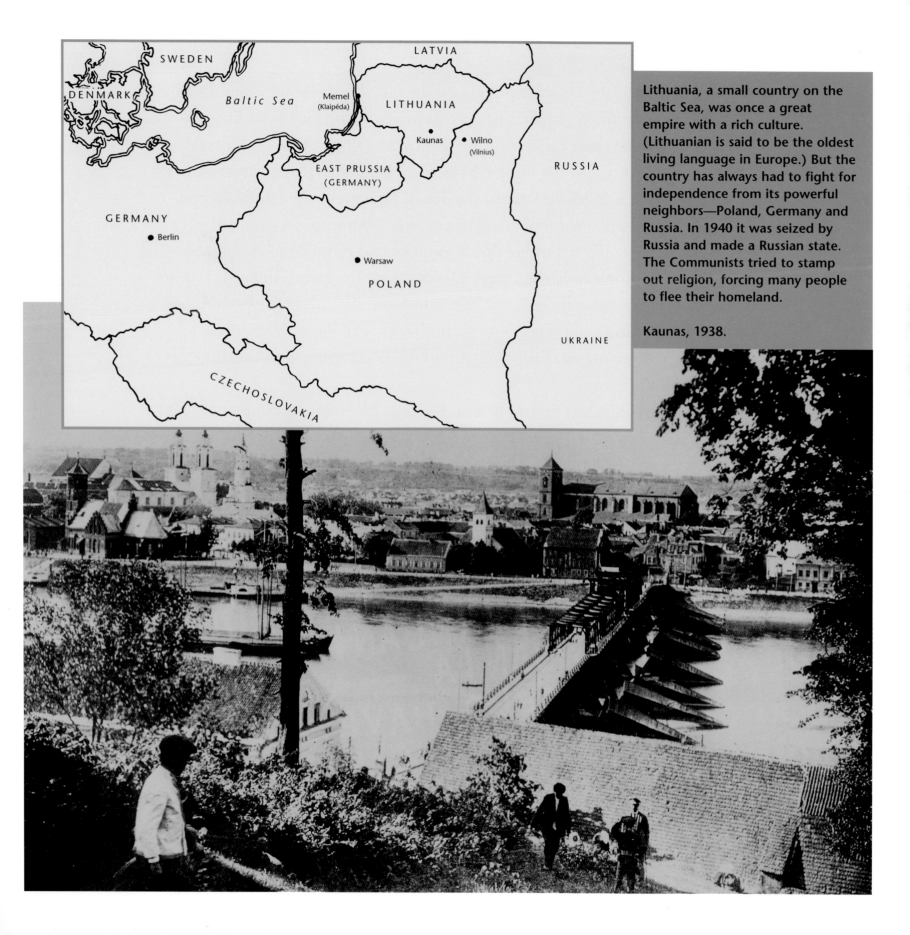

Lithuania, a small country on the Baltic Sea, was once a great empire with a rich culture. (Lithuanian is said to be the oldest living language in Europe.) But the country has always had to fight for independence from its powerful neighbors—Poland, Germany and Russia. In 1940 it was seized by Russia and made a Russian state. The Communists tried to stamp out religion, forcing many people to flee their homeland.

Kaunas, 1938.

IGOR peered at the large map lying on the table in the hotel room. Each country was outlined in pale colors crisscrossed with black lines that showed the roads and railroads. Lithuania was a tiny yellow blob bordering the Baltic Sea. But the biggest expanse belonged to Russia, its pink borders stretching east all the way to the Sea of Japan and the Pacific Ocean.

Father had explained that going to Canada would not be easy. All over Europe, borders were shutting down as more and more countries joined the war. The Kaplans needed written permission to leave Lithuania, but no one would give them these visas. Without them, they were trapped in their own country, and time was running out.

Then, in late August, Father burst into the hotel room, and this time his face was full of hope.

"There is a Japanese consul here in Kaunas. His name is Sugihara. They say he has been giving Jews transit visas to leave Russia and enter Japan."

Father grasped Igor's shoulder and squeezed it hard.

"Maybe Mr. Sugihara can help us, too," he said.

Jews were removed from their homes and taken to prison camps.

Juden nicht zugänglich

IGOR'S heart sank as he trudged up the hill to the Japanese consulate. Hundreds of people were clustered outside the black iron fence surrounding the white house. Father said that many of these people had been waiting for weeks, hoping to get a visa from Mr. Sugihara.

Across from the consulate was a park. As they passed it, Igor noticed a sign posted on the fence: NO JEWS ALLOWED.

Just then, at the side of the house, a gate opened, and a large black Buick drove out. The car moved slowly past the Kaplan family. It was driven by a weary-looking Japanese man.

"Stop!" Igor's father shouted, and he ran after the car. He caught up and banged on the window. The man rolled it down. It was Mr. Sugihara.

Anti-semitism, or prejudice against Jews, has always existed. But even though Jews had suffered persecution for centuries, the German Nazis carried this persecution to its greatest extreme. They tried to rid Europe of Jews. This period in history came to be called the Holocaust.

15

"Please," Bernard Kaplan begged, and he held out a form.

"My government has ordered me to issue no more visas," Mr. Sugihara said. Then he noticed Igor and Nomi. They were gripping Mother's hand. He looked into the back seat, where two small boys sat quietly. The car was packed with suitcases and boxes. The Sugiharas were leaving.

Mr. Sugihara wrote something on the form, then pulled out a bright red stamp and stamped the paper.

"Good-bye," he nodded, and he rolled up the window. As the Buick disappeared down the street, Igor saw the faces of the boys pressed against the back window.

17

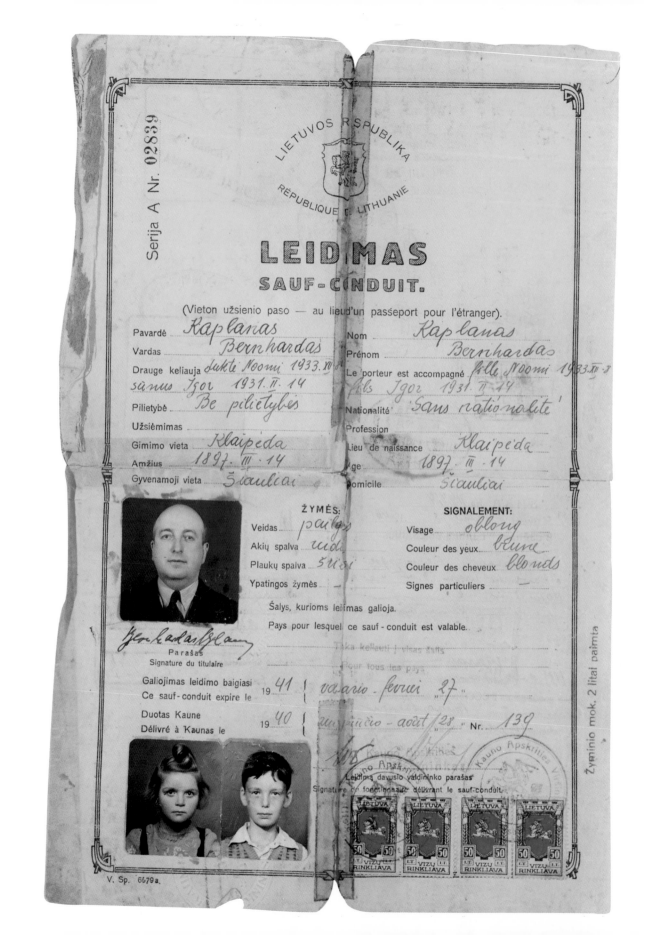

Serija A Nr. 02839

LIETUVOS RESPUBLIKA

RÉPUBLIQUE DE LITHUANIE

LEIDIMAS
SAUF-CONDUIT.

(Vieton užsienio paso — au lieud'un passéport pour l'étranger).

Pavardė	*Kaplanas*	Nom	*Kaplanas*
Vardas	*Bernhardas*	Prénom	*Bernhardas*
Drauge keliauja	*duktė Noomi 1933.IV.8*	Le porteur est accompagné	*fille Noomi 1933.IV.8*
	sūnus Igor 1931.II.14		*fils Igor 1931.II.14*
Pilietybė	*Be pilietybės*	Nationalité	*Sans nationalité*
Užsiėmimas		Profession	
Gimimo vieta	*Klaipėda*	Lieu de naissance	*Klaipėda*
Amžius	*1897.III.14*	Age	*1897.III.14*
Gyvenamoji vieta	*Šiauliai*	Domicile	*Šiauliai*

ŽYMĖS:		SIGNALEMENT:	
Veidas	*pailgas*	Visage	*oblong*
Akių spalva	*ruda*	Couleur des yeux	*brune*
Plaukų spalva	*šviesi*	Couleur des cheveux	*blonds*
Ypatingos žymės	—	Signes particuliers	—

Šalys, kurioms leidimas galioja.

Pays pour lesquel ce sauf-conduit est valable.

Tinka keliauti į visas šalis

Pour tous les pays

Bernhardas Kaplan
Parašas
Signature du titulaire

Galiojimas leidimo baigiasi	19 *41*	*vasario – février* "*27*"	
Ce sauf-conduit expire le			
Duotas Kaune	19 *40*	*rugpjūčio – août* "*28*"	Nr. *139*
Délivré à Kaunas le			

Leidimą davusio valdininko parašas
Signature du fonctionnaire délivrant le sauf-conduit.

Žyminio mok. 2 litai paimta

V. Sp. 6679 a.

The visa that allowed Bernard, Igor and Nomi Kaplan to escape.

Chiune Sugihara had just been appointed Japanese consul in Kaunas when thousands of Jews began asking him for visas that would allow them to leave Russia and enter Japan. From there they hoped to cross the ocean to seek new lives in North America or Australia. Desperate to get out of Lithuania before Hitler's advance, they lined up outside the consulate gates day and night.

Against his government's orders, Sugihara wrote out as many as three hundred visas a day, allowing thousands of people to escape certain death. He had been raised in the Samurai tradition, he said, of helping those in need.

On the day the Kaplans received their visas, Sugihara and his family left the consulate. He had been told to close down the office. He eventually died in disgrace for disobeying orders, but he never regretted what he had done. In 1985 he was named a Righteous Gentile by the government of Israel — an award given to non-Jews who helped save Jewish people during the war.

Top: Chiune Sugihara with his family.

Bottom: Refugees outside the Japanese consulate in Kaunas.

Igor hurriedly packed his bag as soon as they returned to the hotel. He was anxious to leave.

But his parents huddled around the table, talking quietly. They sent Nomi to bed.

Igor couldn't understand it. They had their papers now. Hitler's troops were getting closer. Why were they waiting?

Then Father explained. The papers were only good for him and the two children, who traveled on their father's passport. But Mother was Russian. She needed separate permission to leave Lithuania.

Day after day she tried to get a visa from the Russian consulate. But the answer was always no. "Why would you want to leave?" the official would ask.

Two weeks passed. Igor saw the black headlines at the newsstand. The German troops were advancing.

Finally they could wait no longer.

"You must go without me," Mother said. Nomi began to cry. Mother bent down to give her a hug. "I won't give up," she promised. "I'm going back to the consulate. As soon as I get my papers, I'll follow you." But when Igor kissed his mother good-bye, she hugged him so hard that he could scarcely breathe. And he was suddenly afraid that he might never see her again.

THE next afternoon, Igor, Nomi and Father were at the Kaunas train station. They loaded their bags and then stood on the platform and waited. The engine blew a blast of steam. The conductor waved at them impatiently. They would have to get on board.

On the train, Igor stopped in the corridor while impatient passengers

tried to squeeze by behind him. He pressed against the window, looking
down the platform. The crowds had thinned.

The whistle blew. The steam cleared.

A woman ran down the platform, waving a paper in her hand.

"There she is!" he shouted. It was Mother.

During World War II it was dangerous and difficult being a Jew. As more and more of Europe was conquered by Germany, the rest of the world shut down its borders. Most barred the entry of Jewish refugees.

No one could leave or enter a country without official papers. These visas, or letters of transit, were not only very difficult to obtain, but they were often stolen, bought and sold by dishonest officials. The papers were more valuable than money. For Jews, they meant the difference between life and death.

One day after Nadja Kaplan received permission to leave Lithuania, the borders closed for good. Most Jews did not get out in time. Families were split up and sent to concentration camps. By the end of the war, ninety percent of Lithuania's Jewish community (more than 130,000 people) had been killed by the Nazis.

One of the tragedies of the war was that children as well as adults were put in concentration camps.

THE train lurched out of the station. Igor and Nomi leaned against Mother and watched the countryside slip by. Mother and Father sat quietly. Igor knew they were still worried. Mother's papers only allowed her to leave Lithuania. In Russia she would have to go to the Japanese embassy to try to get permission to enter Japan with the rest of the family.

Before long the train came to a stop. Igor pulled out his map and ran his finger along the line that marked the railway. They were at the border between Lithuania and Russia.

An officer opened the door.

"Papers," he demanded.

Father took out their papers and the officer examined them carefully. Igor could hear his mother's heart beating. She was very still.

The man looked at the papers for a long time. Then he handed them back. Other officials made them open their luggage. Some of the suitcases contained Mother's amber jewelry and family photographs in silver frames. The officials took those suitcases away.

"You can pick them up in Moscow," they said.

It was night when they arrived in Moscow. Mother went straight to the station master.

"Where are our missing suitcases?" she asked.

But the station master only laughed.

The Kremlin.

THE next morning, Igor, Nomi and Father toured Moscow, the capital of Russia. On Igor's map the city was just a round dot, like the center of a wheel where the spokes of roads and railways met. But it was the biggest city he had ever seen, its buildings and squares grand and imposing.

They walked down the vast parade ground of Red Square. They admired St. Basil's Cathedral sitting at one end of the square like a shining pink fairy castle. They walked around the walls of the Kremlin, Moscow's old fortress.

Lenin's tomb.

All day Igor thought of his mother at the Japanese embassy. He imagined her seeing a gentle man like Mr. Sugihara, who would sign her papers with a few quick brush strokes and press on the bright red stamp.

But when they met her back at the train station, she was empty-handed.

"The emperor of Japan has ordered no more visas," she said. "The officials here are not like Mr. Sugihara. They are not prepared to disobey their government."

The trainman leaned out of the car and waved his yellow flag. The Trans-Siberian Express, the train that would take them to the other end of Russia, was ready to leave.

"We cannot wait," said Father. "We have tickets for this train. We must get as far as we can and hope for the best."

Igor had never been on a train like the Trans-Siberian Express. The family had their own compartment – a small room with seats that turned into bunk beds at night.

Igor spent hours with his nose pressed against the train window, watching the countryside slide by. At first the land was flat and covered with trees. Every so often a village appeared. Igor saw farmers eating their lunch in the middle of a field, their bread and soup bowls spread out on a blanket.

After two days, the mountains appeared. On Igor's map they looked like a long snake. Then everything became flat again, and even the people looked different.

"Why does everyone look so strange?" Nomi asked.

The Trans-Siberian Express just before it pulls out of Moscow.

"The Ural Mountains are the dividing line between Europe and Asia," Father explained. "We are now in Asia, so the people are Asian."

THE Ural Mountains faded into the distance. The train crossed a wide river near Cheliabinsk. Igor found it on his map. It was called the Tobol. Yellow birches lined farmers' fields, the black earth dotted with stubble.

S I B E R I A

Moscow

Ural Mountains

Tobol River

Chelyabinsk

Omsk

Novosibirsk

Krasnoyarsk

Irkutsk

Lake Baikal

Chita

Khabarovsk

Ussuri River

Vladivostok

Russia is a vast country — more than twice as big as the United States. It covers about one-sixth of all the land in the world and is home to more than 150 national groups.

The Trans-Siberian Express, the longest railway in the world, runs from Moscow, the capital, to Russia's far-eastern port, Vladivostok. The railway took twenty-six years to build and stretches for almost six thousand miles (9,600 kilometers), cutting through mountains, spanning rivers and crossing permafrost. In 1940, the complete trip took ten days.

Igor met Felix Fogelman just a day after the train left Moscow. The Fogelmans were on their way to Shanghai, China. From there they hoped to start a new life in Australia.

IGOR rapped smartly on the door of the next compartment. He shuffled his feet impatiently. It was a long time before Mr. Fogelman's frightened face appeared at the door.

"Ah, it's you, Igor," he said. Behind him, Mrs. Fogelman smiled stiffly. Felix stood up happily and joined Igor in the corridor.

"Off to do more exploring, are you? I should think you two know every inch of this train by now. Try not to bother the other passengers. And please be back in one hour," Mr. Fogelman called after them.

But the boys had already disappeared down the corridor, laughing and shoving each other as the roll of the train bumped them from side to side.

It was fun having a friend right next door. Igor and Felix met every day and never got tired of exploring the train. They walked through the second-class carriage where people sat crowded together on hard benches. They tiptoed through the quieter first-class cars that had soft seats for people who had paid more money. The lucky ones, like the Fogelmans and

the Kaplans, had their own compartments.

The boys made friends with the waiters in the dining cars. They followed attendants down the corridors as they delivered glasses of tea. They traced their route on Igor's map. And they spent endless hours looking out the window.

They saw goat herds grazing in the hills outside Novosibirsk and tried to see how many they could count before the train passed. Igor always counted the white goats and Felix always got the black ones. They woke up early and looked into the lighted windows of the houses they passed, watching sleepy families eating breakfast. They made plans to celebrate Rosh Hashanah together on the train.

It was so much fun, Igor almost forgot about the war. The train felt like a cozy cocoon that was speeding them away to freedom.

THEN, one night, when the train was stopped just outside the city of
Irkutsk on Lake Baikal, two men in dark suits came on board.

"Papers," they demanded, knocking on the Kaplans' compartment door.
Father produced his papers. Again the officials seemed to examine them for
too long before handing them back and moving down the corridor.

Igor heard the knock on the Fogelmans' door. There was silence, then
talking, then more silence. He heard a flurry of sounds – angry words,
doors closing, hurried footsteps.

Igor opened the door. Nomi followed him out into the corridor. It was empty. A whistle blew. Igor rushed to the window.

Outside, the Fogelmans were being led down the platform. As the train began to move, Felix turned back to look at his friends, his eyes dark pools of confusion and fear.

Igor felt his mother's hand on his shoulder.

"From now on," she said, "you must stay here in the compartment. You are not to talk to anyone."

She pulled them back into the compartment, and the door slid closed in front of Igor's face.

IGOR lost track of the days. Rosh Hashanah and Yom Kippur came and went. There was no celebration.

"Will we be safe when we get to the sea?" Nomi asked. She was sucking her thumb and lying on the seat staring at the ceiling. She wasn't terribly interested in the view.

Igor shook his head. "I don't know," he said. "The war is everywhere."

The nights suddenly grew very cold, and the forests were tinged with frost. On his map, Igor could see that the train was heading almost straight north. Then the track curved to the south, following a wide river with thick wooded hills on the other side. Beyond those hills lay China.

Igor leaned his forehead against the train window. They were almost at the end of the line. Soon, Father said, they would be able to smell the sea.

Igor watched the trees flash by. Birches, cedars, oaks...

His eyes opened wide. Ahead, in the water on the far side of the river, he saw a large, pale shape. It was a tiger, standing in the brown water up to its belly, its coat long and thick, its eyes yellow and unblinking.

It was gone so quickly, Igor almost thought he had imagined it.

Siberia is the name given to Russia east of the Ural Mountains — the Asian part of Russia. A vast wilderness, it contains forests, grasslands (steppes) and mountains. It is rich in wildlife, including bears, lynxes, wolves, fox and ermine.

The rare Siberian tiger hunts in the forests bordering the Ussuri River, near the China-Russia border. It is the largest tiger in the world, capable of eating up to 90 pounds (40 kilograms) of meat at one sitting and able to leap up to 30 feet (10 meters) in a single bound.

The Siberian is a lone hunter and seldom seen, but it loves water and will often drag its dead prey near rivers to eat. In 1920 there were about 100,000 Siberian tigers in the world. Today there are probably no more than 300 left in the wild.

Views of
Vladivostok in the
early 1940s.

VLADIVOSTOK was cold and crowded. Igor stayed very close to his
father as he and Nomi followed him through the streets. They met Mother
outside the Japanese consulate. Nomi rushed into her arms, but Mother
barely seemed to see her. She just looked straight into Father's eyes and
shook her head. She had been refused her visa.

Mother and Father moved to the side of the steps and talked quietly.
Father reached into his coat and pulled out an envelope. Mother shook her
head and began to cry. He pressed it into her hands. Mother looked at
Igor and Nomi for a long time. Then she put the envelope in her pocket
and went back into the consulate.

Igor knew what the envelope contained. It was their money, the money for their new life in Canada.

He sat down on the steps. Nomi collected colorful leaves off the streets, but Igor felt frozen inside.

What would happen if the officials took the money and still didn't give Mother her visa? He knew such things happened.

He looked around at Vladivostok, hemmed in by dark hills and the icy harbor. Naval vessels, tugboats and whaling ships crowded the stone piers. The air was filled with the sharp smells of seaweed and sawdust and the sounds of many languages that Igor had never heard before – Japanese, Korean, Chinese. Sailors, fishermen and dock workers milled in the narrow streets. He saw no other children.

It was the most unfriendly city Igor had ever seen. How could they stay here? Where else could they go? They had reached the very end of the continent. Only the sea lay in front of them.

Father and Nomi sat down beside him. A cold wind began to blow down from the hills. Igor curled up against his father and fell asleep. He hadn't done that since he was little.

It was almost dark when Mother came out of the building. She was smiling wearily. She had her visa, and they were all finally free to leave Russia.

But the envelope with the money was gone and, later, Igor noticed that his mother was no longer wearing her wedding ring.

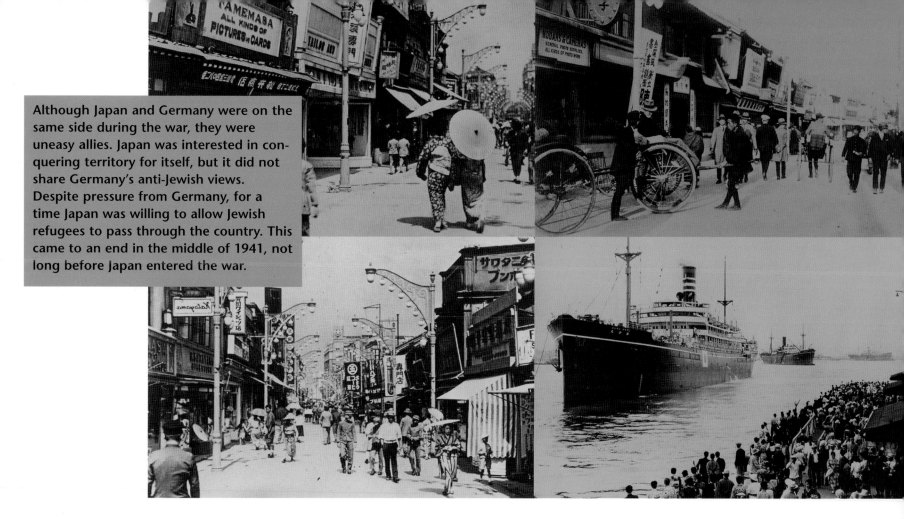

Although Japan and Germany were on the same side during the war, they were uneasy allies. Japan was interested in conquering territory for itself, but it did not share Germany's anti-Jewish views. Despite pressure from Germany, for a time Japan was willing to allow Jewish refugees to pass through the country. This came to an end in the middle of 1941, not long before Japan entered the war.

Kobe, Japan, in the 1940s.

"EAT," Mother said, pointing to the tray on the low table. "You must get your strength back, after being so ill."

They were in a small inn in Kobe, Japan, waiting for their ship to leave for Canada. They had boarded a tramp steamer in Vladivostok, and the crossing to Japan had been crowded and noisy. The trip took several days longer than usual because of the stormy weather. Igor could still feel the lurching rise and fall of the boat. He'd been seasick for the whole trip.

He pushed a few grains of rice into his mouth. The food was so strange – rice and raw fish and smelly, bright yellow pickles. The tea tasted funny. There were no forks or spoons. The cups had no handles.

He shoved his bowl away. The delicate porcelain tipped on its tiny base and slipped to the floor and broke.

Father looked at Igor sternly, but he was too tired himself to be angry. Igor stared at the floor so Nomi wouldn't see his tears.

45

There was a gentle knock outside the room. Father stood up and slid aside the panelled door. Two Japanese women, their heads low, handed him a bundle wrapped in a cloth.

"For the children," they said, bowing to Igor and Nomi. Then they

bowed again and slipped softly away.

Father brought the bundle into the room and untied the cloth. Igor's eyes lit up when he saw what was inside.

It was a basket filled with oranges, apples and bread.

THE *Empress of Russia* looked dressed for war, Igor thought. The ship sat in Kobe harbor, her long hull painted with ugly zigzagged stripes. She was even fitted with guns. Inside, however, she was still a passenger liner, with cabins and dining rooms.

The voyage to Canada took seven days. Igor hated it. There was nothing to do, and Mother and Father had no money left for treats. There were no cities to look for on his map, no rivers or mountains to mark their route.

Canada declared war on Germany in September, 1939, shortly after Germany invaded Poland. Although Canada was never attacked, the country sent troops, weapons, aircraft and ships to fight in Europe, North Africa and in the Pacific. Passenger liners like the *Empress of Russia* were converted into troop ships and stood by ready for action.

Canadian passenger ship outfitted for troop transport.

Igor tried to teach Nomi how to play chess, but all she wanted to do was tuck the pieces into bed like little doll families. One of the other passengers taught him a card game called solitaire, but it was boring and stupid. Most of the ship's attendants spoke English, and it sounded harsh and loud to Igor's ears. How would he ever learn enough of the language to go to school in Canada? How would he ever make a new friend?

He missed Felix. He missed the train, where he could watch the world slide by like a constantly changing film. On the ocean there was nothing to see. Just endless water stretching out in all directions.

In the middle of one night, the ship's sirens sounded. They blasted through Igor's dreams like a moan and a scream at the same time. Igor heard running footsteps in the corridor. Mother made him put on his coat and boots over his pajamas, and they all put on lifejackets.

Up on the deck, passengers clustered around the lifeboats. Igor tried to count them. So many people. Was there enough room in the lifeboats for all of them?

The sirens stopped. Silence settled over the ship for a brief moment before the passengers began talking again and headed back to their cabins.

"Why did they wake us up?" Nomi asked.

"Canada is at war with Germany, too. There are German submarines and warships everywhere. The captain must have thought we were being attacked."

"Will we ever be safe?" Nomi asked.

"In Canada," her brother said. "In Canada we will be safe."

Vancouver, in
the early 1940s.

VANCOUVER shimmered like a jewel in the October sunlight. White-capped mountains rose up behind the city.

"Papers, please."

Out of habit, Igor stiffened when the immigration officer came on board and asked to see their documents. They were tattered from being folded and pulled out so many times.

He held his breath while the officer scanned the papers carefully, looking at each of their faces in turn. Igor wondered whether he still looked anything like the solemn boy in the photo on his father's passport. He felt as if he had left that boy far behind in the turret house in Memel.

Like a hammer the official stamp came down on the passport. The immigration officer waved the family through.

"Welcome to Canada," he said, smiling.

IGOR watched the raindrops race down the train window. His reflection stared back at him. His hair needed cutting. His jacket was rumpled and smelled like coal dust. He looked down and brushed at a stain on the sleeve. He knew it would be a long time before Mother and Father would be able to buy him new clothes.

They were on the last leg of their journey on a train that was carrying them across Canada to Ontario, where Oma and Opa lived. Igor marked the strange-sounding places they passed. Kicking Horse Pass. Moose Jaw. Portage la Prairie.

This time there was no compartment with seats that turned into bunks. There were no nice meals in the dining car. Igor got a job helping the man who ran the bar. He cleared dishes and wiped the tables. The waiters helped him with his English. His pay was one cheese sandwich a day.

Igor watched the new country roll by. Sometimes he almost felt as if he were back in Russia. There were mountains, only this time they were the towering, ice-covered Rockies, not the gently rounded Urals. There were long stretches of prairie, flat as a table just like the steppes of western Siberia. Finally the train chugged through the swamps, lakes and thick forests of northern Ontario. It looked just like the Russian taiga, where the fir trees crowded in close to the tracks.

But in one way this train ride was very different. In Russia they had been running away. Now they were going to their new home. They had traveled almost three-quarters of the way around the globe. It had been a long journey.

Soon they would arrive in Cornwall in eastern Ontario. Oma and Opa would meet them at the station.

And this time when they stepped off the train, it would be for the last time.

EPILOGUE

Igor Kaplan and his family settled on an abandoned farm just outside Cornwall, Ontario. It was a condition of their immigration that they spend at least a year working the land, but they had never farmed before, and they knew nothing about growing crops or raising livestock. Igor and Nomi went to the local school and learned to speak English in three months.

After a year, the family moved to Windsor, Ontario, where Nadja Kaplan opened a photography studio and the family began a new life. There were some difficult times ahead for the Kaplans, but overall the family prospered in Canada, a country they quickly came to love. Igor became a lawyer. Nomi became an artist.

As the war continued in Europe, they learned that they were among the last Jews to escape through Russia and Japan. By the time World War II was over in 1945, six million Jews had died in the Holocaust.

Young concentration camp survivors freed after liberation by the Allied army at the end of the war.

The Kaplans on their farm north of Cornwall, Ontario.

Glossary

ally – A person or country that joins another for a common purpose, such as fighting on the same side in a war.

amber – A clear yellow tree gum that has hardened into a fossil and is often used in jewelry. Mines in Lithuania and other countries along the Baltic Sea produce 90 percent of the world's amber.

Buick – An American make of car.

Communists – Those who agree with the ideas of Karl Marx. Communists are opposed to private enterprise, believing instead that workers should own the "means of production."

concentration camp – A place where political prisoners are kept and, during World War II, were murdered.

consul – An official who looks after his or her country's and citizens' interests within another country. A consulate is the building where a consul works and often lives.

embassy – The office of the ambassador, a diplomat working in another country to represent the home country or government.

gentile – A non-Jewish person.

Holocaust – The mass destruction of Jews by the Nazis during World War II.

immigration – Moving to a foreign country as a permanent resident.

Nazi – A member of the German National Socialist Party, or someone who holds similar opinions, such as the view that some races are superior to others.

Oma / Opa – German for Grandma and Grandpa.

passport – An official document that establishes identity and citizenship; it is required when traveling to foreign countries.

permafrost – Soil that remains frozen all year long.

pier – A long structure running out into the sea to serve as a landing place for ships.

porcelain – Delicate, glazed pottery.

refugee – Someone who flees his or her home country because of persecution, war or disaster and seeks safety in another country.

Rosh Hashanah – The Jewish New Year celebration.

samurai – A Japanese warrior.

steppes – The flat grassy treeless plains of Russia.

synagogue – A Jewish temple.

taiga – The northern coniferous forest area of Russia.

tramp steamer – A ship that carries freight but runs on no regular route or schedule.

turret – A small tower.

visa – An official document or stamp that allows the holder to enter or leave a country.

Yom Kippur – A solemn Jewish holiday that is marked by fasting and repentance.

Picture Credits

Title page: UPI/CORBIS-BETTMANN. Page 10 (top left): William Kaplan. Page 10 (bottom left and right): UPI/CORBIS-BETTMANN. Page 11 (top): National Archives, courtesy of the United States Holocaust Memorial Museum (USHMM) Photo Archives. Page 11 (bottom): Jerzy Tomaszewski, courtesy of USHMM Photo Archives. Page 12 (left): National Archives, courtesy of USHMM Photo Archives. Page 12 (center): Bundesarchiv, courtesy of USHMM Photo Archives. Page 12 (right): Ghetto Fighters' House, courtesy of USHMM Photo Archives. Page 13: UPI/CORBIS-BETTMANN. Page 15 (left): Jerzy Tomaszewski, courtesy of USHMM Photo Archives. Page 15 (right): Yad Vashem Photo Archives, courtesy of USHMM Photo Archives. Pages 18-19: William Kaplan. Page 20 (both): Hiroki Sugihara/Visas for Life Foundation. Page 24: Yad Vashem Photo Archives, courtesy of USHMM Photo Archives. Page 25: Yad Vashem Photo Archives, courtesy of USHMM Photo Archives.

Page 26: William Kaplan. Page 28: UPI/CORBIS-BETTMANN. Page 29: UPI/CORBIS-BETTMANN. Page 30: UPI/CORBIS-BETTMANN. Page 31 (top): Tim Gibson/Envision. Page 31 (bottom): Jerry Kobalenko/First Light. Page 32: UPI/CORBIS-BETTMANN. Page 36: 1997 James Balog. Page 41 (background): Jerry Kobalenko/First Light. Page 41 (left): Dick Haneda/ The Toronto Zoo. Page 41 (right): Gary Crandall/Envision. Page 42 (all): UPI/CORBIS-BETTMANN. Page 45 (all): UPI/CORBIS-BETTMANN. Page 50: Canadian Pacific Archives. Page 52: City of Vancouver Archives. Page 53: Canadian Pacific Archives. Page 55 (both): Courtesy of CN. Page 58 (left): Documentary Film Archives, courtesy of Photo Archives. Page 58 (right): National Archives, courtesy of USHMM Photo Archives. Page 59: William Kaplan.

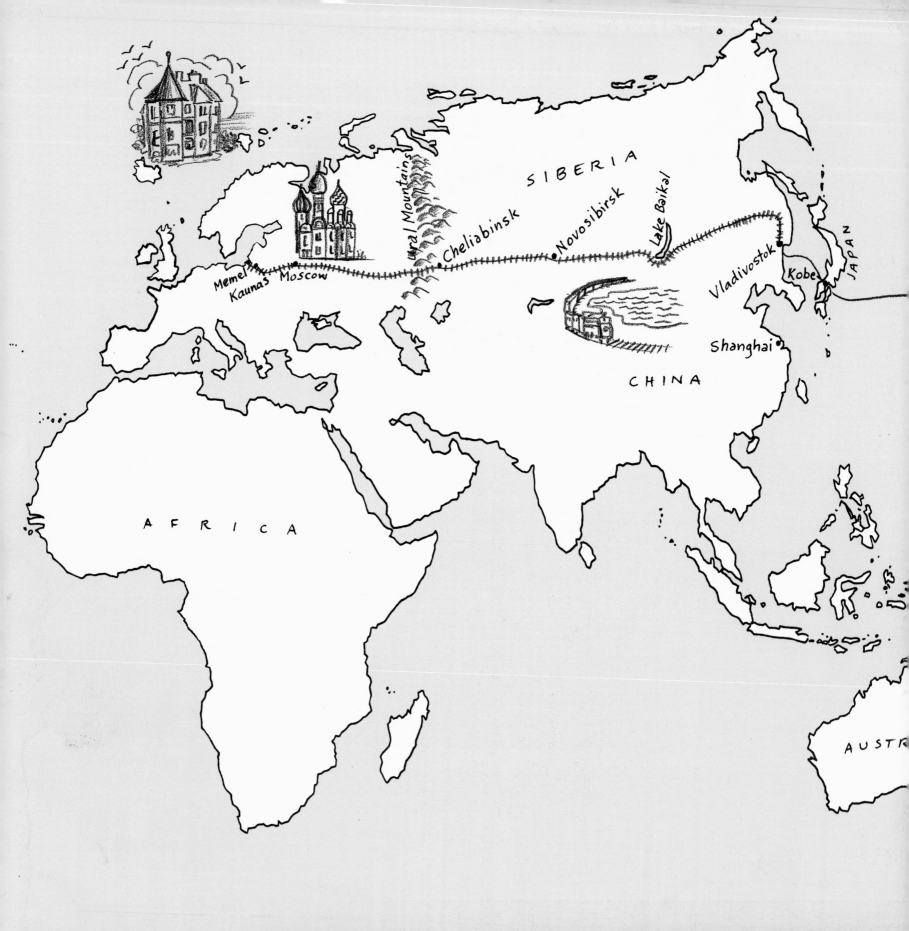

SIBERIA

Ural Mountains

Cheliabinsk   Novosibirsk   Lake Baikal

Memel
Kaunas   Moscow

Vladivostok   Kobe

JAPAN

Shanghai

CHINA

AFRICA

AUSTR